Career Exploration

Careers If You Like Research and Analysis

Barbara Sheen

ReferencePoint Press®

San Diego, CA

About the Author

Barbara Sheen is the author of 103 books for young people. She lives in New Mexico with her family. In her spare time, she likes to swim, walk, garden, and cook.

For more information, contact:
ReferencePoint Press, Inc.
PO Box 27779
San Diego, CA 92198
www.ReferencePointPress.com

Picture Credits:

Cover: Undrey/Shutterstock.com

19: chudakov2/Shutterstock.com
26: poba/iStockphoto.com
34: Mario Anzuoni/Reuters/Newscom
64: gradyreese/iStockphoto.com

LIBRARY OF CONGRESS CATALOGING-IN-PUBLICATION DATA

Name: Sheen, Barbara, author.
Title: Careers If You Like Research and Analysis/By Barbara Sheen.
Description: San Diego, CA: ReferencePoint Press, Inc., 2020. | Series:
  Career Exploration | Includes bibliographical references and index. |
  Audience: Grade 9 to 12. |
Identifiers: LCCN 2019011109 (print) | LCCN 2019018029 (ebook) | ISBN
  9781682825921 (eBook) | ISBN 9781682825914 (hardback)
Subjects: LCSH: Science—Vocational guidance—Juvenile literature. |
  Research—Vocational guidance—Juvenile literature. | Vocational
  guidance—Juvenile literature.
Classification: LCC Q147 (ebook) | LCC Q147 .S49 2020 (print) | DDC
  001.4023—dc23
LC record available at https://lccn.loc.gov/2019011109

Contents

Choosing a Career

Choosing a career is a major life decision. But how do you do so when, according to the Bureau of Labor Statistics, there are approximately twelve thousand occupations to choose from? Although having tons of choices sounds good, being confronted by seemingly endless possibilities can be overwhelming. Often, the more choices a person has, the harder it is to make a decision. In fact, having too many options can be paralyzing and can cause stress and anxiety. Plus, who has the time to investigate thousands of different careers? And even if a career sounds appealing, how do you know it is right for you? As author and psychologist Barry Schwartz explains,

> As the number of options increases, the costs, in time and effort, of gathering the information needed to make a good choice also increase. The level of certainty people have about their choice decreases. And the anticipation that they will regret their choice increases.[1]

Narrowing Down Your Options

So how do you narrow down your options without missing out on your dream job? One good way is to identify the things you like to do, determine why you enjoy doing them, and then explore careers that involve the tasks you like. Generally, people who pursue careers that involve doing things that genuinely interest them are happier, more motivated, and more productive than those who do not. Therefore, they are more likely to advance in their chosen field. Indeed, since the average person spends approximately 120,000 hours at work in a lifetime, what could be better than spending all these hours being paid to do something you love? As author and career coach Lori Bumgarner explains,

> There's nothing more life-draining than being stuck in a job that doesn't bring us some form of joy and doesn't utilize our strengths and interests. . . . When we're doing what we love, we can't help but excel and grow in our area of expertise. This can lead to rapid promotion and career success.[2]

Sometimes it is easy to identify the things you like to do. Ideally, your hobbies and favorite activities have lots in common. Not everyone's favorite activities seem closely related. But if you look more closely, you might be surprised to learn that even seemingly diverse activities have more in common than you realized. For instance, say your favorite activities include reading mystery novels and watching crime programs (because you love gathering clues and figuring out "who done it"), participating in a service project in which you test and analyze the water quality in a local stream, planning a fantasy football team, and comparison shopping on the web. Although these activities seem unrelated, they all involve uncovering and collecting information, then reviewing the information in order to draw an informed conclusion and/or solve a problem. Or to put it more simply, they involve research and analysis. If many of your favorite activities also involve gathering and analyzing information, it makes sense to narrow down your career exploration to occupations that feature research and analysis.

Not Just Hard Science

Although some people think that only STEM careers involve research and analysis, this is not true. You do not have to be a mad scientist or a mathematical whiz to pursue a career that entails research and analysis (although you could be). Careers that incorporate research and analysis as a regular part of the job encompass many different industries. Many of these occupations, such as microbiologist, wildlife scientist, statistician, and computer information research scientist, do focus on science or math. Others, such as economist, historian, anthropologist, sociologist, and political scientist, emphasize the social sciences. Still others have to do with business, law enforcement, teaching, and library science. These include a career as a private investigator, librarian, and college professor, among others.

Because jobs that involve research and analysis span multiple fields, if you have a particular area of interest, you can combine your passions. For instance, if you love books almost as much as you love doing research, you could become a librarian; if the world of finance fascinates you, you could become a financial research analyst. And because your job allows you to do things that you like, the path you choose should lead to personal fulfillment and professional success. "Work," advises writer Siobhan Harmer, "doesn't have to be something that you hate doing, stay true to yourself and always do what makes you happy."[3]

Data Analyst

What Does a Data Analyst Do?

Data analysts collect, search through, organize, and analyze numerical and less structured data such as surveys and opinion polls in order to extract information that helps businesses, health and educational institutions, the government, and other organizations solve problems and make decisions about the future. Data analysts spot and monitor patterns and trends; determine consumer, audience, and voter likes and dislikes; pinpoint specific markets and prices for products and services; and identify the effectiveness of marketing campaigns, teaching methods, and medical treatments, among other things. Data analysts also develop systems for collecting data and design and maintain databases.

Part statistician, part detective, and part computer whiz, these men and women examine mountains of data in an effort to identify relevant information. This requires lots of time, patience, and care. As Robert Roser, head of the Scientific Computing Division at Fermilab in Batavia, Illinois, explains, "We are looking for that handful of data that is meaningful for what we are doing."[4]

Once these experts have identified applicable data, they use statistics and specialized software to help analyze it. Then analysts translate their findings into written reports and visual aids such as charts, graphs, tables, and spreadsheets, in a way that decision makers can understand. This last step is vital. "If you can't express your results in an easily-understood and credible manner, well, you're in trouble,"[5] says data analyst and blogger Peter Hsu.

Data analysts work in almost every industry. Depending on their employer, they may be known as data analysts or may have a title specific to the industry they work in. For instance, data analysts known as market research analysts, operational research analysts, and business analysts specialize in the world of business, while scientific data analysts specialize in working with data related to scientific and medical research. Since data analysts work in many career fields, if you decide to pursue this occupation and have a special area of interest, you can combine your love for research and analysis with your other passions. Sports fans, for example, can work in sports analytics providing professional and collegiate teams with information related to player recruitment, game strategy and tactics, and sports merchandising. Those concerned with social justice can work for government agencies analyzing data with the aim of providing solutions to issues related to immigration, economics, crime, and the environment.

A Typical Workday

Data analysts also spend a good part of every workday designing, programming, and running data-collecting systems. These are computer applications that facilitate the collection and organization of specific data. Analysts also develop, set up, and maintain simplified databases, which serve as tools for nonanalysts. Writing reports and creating visual aids, which they present to management, clients, and other interested parties, also fills their time. Attending lots of meetings and working closely with other professionals—such as information technology personnel, advertising and marketing professionals, scientific research teams, engineers, and company executives—are other common activities.

Statistics Are Important

"Reporting and analyzing the performance of a [marketing] campaign is just as important as campaign implementation. Without performance statistics, there's no way of knowing whether or not your marketing activity has been successful—and to what extent. To report on the performance of a campaign, you typically have to go to multiple sources, download the data from each into a spreadsheet, then arrange the data to produce graphs and metrics that are easily digestible."

—Adam Read, senior data analyst at Further Digital Marketing Limited, London, England

Adam Read, "Answering Difficult Questions: A Day in the Life of a Data Analyst," Further, September 6, 2017. www.further.co.uk.

As Eric Fandel, a data analyst at a mobile marketing technology company, explains, "I work very closely with the Product and Engineering teams . . . reporting on the success of product updates help these teams make educated decisions every day. I also pull specific reports for the executive team."[6]

Education and Training

If your goal is to become a data analyst, you'll need a bachelor's degree. You can start preparing for this career in high school by taking math and statistics classes. Data analysts use math and statistics on a daily basis. They rely on their knowledge of both to understand statistical software and to construct graphs, tables, and spreadsheets. These classes also help students develop analytic and problem-solving skills, which are essential to this job.

Computer science classes are also important. Data analysts depend on their computer skills to use complex software and create databases. But even the most tech-savvy individuals are unlikely to succeed in this career unless they can present complex

A Big Job

"Analysts support various things. Some of us focus on helping to decide the best metrics to track; some of us focus on conducting tests for product/marketing campaign improvement. Generally, we translate raw data into understandable, extendable dashboards/reports, so that functional teams [teams consisting of nonanalyst colleagues] can extract useful insights from them. At the same time, we also need to make sure they take actions by solid quantitative basis instead of pure instinct."

—Peter Hsu, data analyst at Carousell Classified Market Place, Singapore

Peter Hsu, "A Day in the Life of a Data Analyst," Carousell, June 27, 2017. https://blog .carousell.com.

information in laypersons' terms. As Jess Kendra, a data analytics manager at a New York public relations firm, explains,

> Successful data analysts understand how to create narratives with data. To remain valuable, the reports, answers and insights data analysis provides have to be understood by the next decision-maker, who frequently is not an analyst.[7]

This is where journalism, drama, and advanced language arts and speech electives come in. These classes teach individuals how to present information clearly.

In college you can choose from among several majors. Data analytics is a relatively new career option; therefore, many colleges do not offer a specific major in this field. Instead, candidates often major in computer science, statistics, math, economics, or finance, all of which can help prepare students for this career. As writer and accountant Greg DePersio explains, "When hiring a data analyst, employers want to see a healthy mix of quantitative acumen [mathematical skill] and computer literacy that goes beyond knowing how to input numbers into Excel."[8]

Skills and Personality

Successful data analysts are highly skilled people. It takes excellent statistical, technical, and analytic skills to get ahead in this career. And these are just some of the skills that are needed. Data analysts must also be curious, persistent, and flexible. They have to sift through loads of data to help their employer make good decisions. Moreover, after hours of research, it is not unusual to hit a dead end and have to begin a new search, which can be challenging for less flexible and less determined individuals. "You have to be willing to dig through the weeds and find answers to complicated questions," advises Fandel. "If you're someone who gives up easily or is not driven to find the solution to a problem, this job might not be for you."[9]

Being knowledgeable about the business or industry they are working for makes it easier for these professionals to identify applicable data, organize it, and analyze it effectively. For example, a data analyst charged with analyzing medical research data would have a hard time doing so unless he or she also has a background in science. Says Erik Berger, a senior web technology manager who's been working in data analysis for more than a decade,

> You obviously need the technical skills to be able to extract data and run statistical analyses, but there is the more intangible ability of finding patterns or irregularities to report on. To be good at it, you need to fully understand the nature of the business that you're analyzing—just looking at the numbers is only half the story.[10]

Great communication and presentation skills are also crucial. For their work to be valuable, data analysts must be able to present their findings simply and clearly. And they must be able to work well with others. "Your success is dependent on your ability to work with people—the people you are gathering the research questions from, peers you collaborate with to execute the work, and the people you deliver the final presentation to,"[11] says Kendra.

Working Conditions

Data analysts work indoors in a comfortable office environment. They spend a great deal of time seated in front of a computer. Most work a traditional five-day, forty-hour week during regular business hours. Occasionally, analysts may have to work overtime to meet deadlines. Depending on the employer and the demands of the project, analysts may work individually or as part of a data analytics team.

Employers and Pay

Data analysts work in virtually every type of business and industry, including manufacturing, health care, financial services, retail, transportation, and media and entertainment, to name a few. Analysts are also employed by government agencies, the military, and educational institutions. Some work for consulting firms that do data analysis for many clients. Thanks to high demand, if you become a data analyst, you can expect to earn a comfortable living. According to Glassdoor, a job and recruiting website, the average annual income for data analysts in 2018 was $83,878, with salaries ranging from about $54,000 to about $107,000. Plus, these professionals usually receive employee benefits that include paid sick and vacation days, health insurance, and retirement benefits.

What Is the Future Outlook for Data Analysts?

Data analytics is a fast-growing field. A joint report by PricewaterhouseCoopers and the Business–Higher Education Forum indicates that by 2021, 69 percent of all employers will seek workers with data analysis skills. Although the Bureau of Labor Statistics does not collect data specifically about data analysts, it predicts that employment opportunities for two types of data analysts—market research analysts and operational research analysts—are expected to increase by 23 and 27 percent, respectively, through 2026, which is faster than average. So if you decide to become a data analyst, you should be welcomed into this hot field.

Find Out More

Digital Analytics Association
401 Edgewater Pl., Suite 600
Wakefield, MA 01880
website: https://community.digitalanalyticsassociation.org

The Digital Analytics Association is an organization dedicated to understanding and improving the study of data collected on websites. It provides job listings, networking opportunities, conferences, articles, a blog, and webinars, and it sponsors a mentoring program for women in technology.

International Institute for Analytics (IIA)
851 SW Sixth Ave., Suite 1025
Portland, OR 97204
website: www.iianalytics.com

The IIA is an independent research firm that works with companies, data analysts, and data scientists to promote, develop, and improve data analysis systems and strategies. It offers an online research library, webinars, blogs, and articles about issues related to data analysis.

Investopedia
114 W. Forty-First St.
New York, NY 10036
website: www.investopedia.com

Investopedia is a website dedicated to helping people understand financial concepts. It provides a variety of articles on many subjects, including articles related to a career as a data analyst, with information about the job, qualifications, educational requirements, career advancement, and pay.

Plus
website: https://plus.maths.org

Plus is an internet magazine that promotes the use of math in careers and daily life. It offers information about different careers involving math, including interviews with data analysts.

Environmental Scientist

What Does an Environmental Scientist Do?

Do you love nature and science? Do you want to make the world a better place? Are you passionate about protecting the earth and human health? If so, you may be interested in a career as an environmental scientist. Environmental scientists use their knowledge of natural science to protect the earth's land, water, air, plants, animals, and people, while taking into account societal needs. As part of their job, these men and women conduct research aimed at identifying, preventing, and/or solving environmental problems. They collect, study, and analyze soil, sediment, air, water, cell, and plant samples in order to identify and assess environmental threats.

Using their findings, environmental scientists develop plans that help prevent and control air and water pollution and soil erosion, protect people and wildlife, minimize human and industrial impact on the environment, and rehabilitate and restore contaminated natural areas, among other things. Their research also helps them identify and design sites for waste disposal and give advice on land use and other governmental policies. Environmental scientists present their findings and recommendations in written reports and scientific journal articles that are often used to advise policy makers, acquire funding for projects, and devise strategies to improve the environment.

Environmental scientists can be generalists who work on all sorts of projects. Or they can be specialists who limit their focus to one particular area of environmental science. These specialists include but are not limited to environmental chemists, who concentrate on studying and minimizing the effects of chemicals on ecosystems; climate change analysts, who look at how the changing climate impacts ecosystems; and environmental health and safety specialists.

A Typical Workday

What environmental scientists do on any given workday varies widely, depending on their area of specialization, employer, and the particular projects they are working on. Indeed, between field studies, lab work, and office duties, no two days are usually alike. "The variation is what makes the job interesting," says Paul Johnston, a member of a team of environmental scientists working for the activist organization Greenpeace.

> In the last fortnight [two-week period] the science unit has looked at pesticides in food, analyzed reports on carbon storage, nitrogen pollution in animal agriculture, modelled air pollution, sampled oceans looking for plastic particles, and done some analysis of hazardous chemicals in children's toys in Russia.[12]

Some days are spent out in the field inspecting sites of proposed projects, monitoring ongoing projects, observing and studying ecosystems, taking notes, testing soil and water, and collecting samples for laboratory study. It is not unusual for fieldwork to take place in remote locations. Nicholas Simpson, a California environmental scientist who helps manage ecosystems located on privately owned timber lands, explains, "My day consists of meeting with foresters and other agency representatives at the closest location we can drive to with a truck, then utilizing all-terrain vehicles and hiking to access remote forest locations."[13]

Other days are spent in laboratories conducting scientific studies or in offices in front of a computer, gathering and analyzing data related to the projects environmental scientists are working on. Writing grant proposals and reports, in which they describe their research and present their recommendations, takes up a good chunk of their time, too.

Education and Training

If you want to become an environmental scientist, you'll need a minimum of a bachelor's degree. Many environmental scientists have advanced degrees. You can start preparing for your future by taking lots of science classes in high school. These will help you become familiar with how scientists think and work, as well as broaden your knowledge of subjects like geology, ecology, biology, and chemistry. Since environmental scientists write lots of reports, taking a journalism class and participating in activities that help you become a better writer, such as working on your school newspaper or yearbook, are also useful. You'll also need to be proficient in a variety of computer programs, so computer science classes are important, too.

At the college level, environmental science is an interdisciplinary major that includes courses in geology, ecology, biology, chemistry, forestry, zoology, and atmospheric science, among other subjects. As part of their studies, students are usually required to do fieldwork and conduct independent research. Martha Mihaltses, a New York environmental scientist, explains, "Off-campus geology and environmental science work provided me with valuable experience in mapping, field identification and sampling. I also worked in a geochemistry lab during the independent research portion of my studies."[14]

In addition to high school and college classes, prospective environmental scientists can learn a lot about what the job entails and gain hands-on experience by joining environmental clubs and/or volunteering for school and community service projects related to the environment. College students can work as summer interns in programs sponsored by various agencies and groups, including the US Environmental Protection Agency (EPA), the National Park Service, and the National Science Foundation. This type of experience helps participants learn practical environmental and research skills, and it looks great on a résumé. "Get as much experience early on as you possibly can," advises California environmental scientist Mia Roberts. "The competition for entry-level . . . jobs can be fierce, and oftentimes it is that little bit of volunteer time you had at that lab, or the summer you spent doing field work banding birds that can make all the difference."[15]

Skills and Personality

Environmental scientists rely on critical-thinking and problem-solving skills to evaluate data and test results, draw logical conclusions, and come up with effective solutions to environmental problems. These professionals also need good writing skills so that they can clearly document their field observations, experiments, and research findings, as well as write reports that can be understood by scientists and nonscientists. "My best advice honestly would be to learn how to write," says EPA environmental scientist Kathryn Snead. "I think no matter what you do in science . . . you're going to need to learn how to write. Even the really technical folks in our labs need to write."[16]

Being motivated, self-disciplined, and able to work both independently and with others are also important traits. Environmental scientists often work in teams with other scientists, technicians, and engineers. So being able to work with and get along with others is essential. Conversely, these professionals also spend time working alone. They must be able to stay on task and get their work done with minimal supervision. This requires focus, motivation, and self-discipline.

Being physically fit is vital, too. Environmental scientists often have to walk long distances and hike and climb through rough terrain, which requires stamina. Lifting and moving heavy equipment may also be a part of the job, so muscular strength comes in handy.

Working Conditions

If you are interested in becoming an environmental scientist, plan on working under a variety of conditions. Environmental scientists work indoors in clean, well-lit laboratories and offices and outdoors in all types of terrain and weather conditions. Depending on the project, environmental scientists may do fieldwork in nearby locations. Or they may work in remote areas for extended periods of time. Mihaltses warns,

> You should expect to get dirty. You should expect to encounter hot, cold, windy, sunny, rainy or even snowy conditions in the field. You learn how to prepare yourself for days out in the field, and how to keep yourself organized and neat, even when conditions don't lend themselves easily to organization.[17]

Most environmental scientists work a traditional forty-hour week during regular business hours. However, when they are doing fieldwork or a lab experiment that requires frequent monitoring, or if an emergency like an oil spill or wildfire occurs, they may work more than the usual forty hours or may have irregular hours.

Employers and Pay

Environmental scientists work for a variety of employers. The largest employers are management, technical, and scientific consulting firms that provide environmental services to businesses and other organizations. Environmental scientists are also employed by local, state, and federal governments; scientific research and development services; social advocacy organizations; architectural and engineering firms; and the gas and petroleum industry.

What you earn in this profession depends on your employer, the location, and your education and experience level. Those with

An environmental scientist collects water samples for testing. Environmental scientists collect, study, and analyze soil, sediment, air, water, cell, and plant samples in order to identify and assess environmental threats.

Responding to Emergencies

"Our primary role at OSPR [California's Office of Spill Prevention and Response] is response to oil spills and although we never look forward to them, the experience can be rewarding (albeit stressful). Spill response allows an opportunity to put our training to use and have a positive influence, hopefully making a bad situation better. . . . All of this work on oil spills is rewarding, especially to see cleaned and rehabilitated wildlife released back into the wild."

—Laird Henkel, senior environmental scientist-supervisor, California Department of Fish and Wildlife

Quoted in California Department of Fish and Wildlife, "Featured Scientist: Laird Henkel," September 5, 2018. www.wildlife.ca.gov.

advanced degrees and senior-level positions can expect to earn more than entry-level employees straight out of college. According to the Bureau of Labor Statistics (BLS), the median annual salary for environmental scientists was $69,400 as of May 2017. The BLS reports that the lowest-paid 10 percent earned less than $41,580, while the highest-paid 10 percent earned more than $122,510. In addition to their pay, most environmental scientists receive employee benefits such as health insurance, paid sick and vacation days, and retirement benefits.

What Is the Future Outlook for Environmental Scientists?

The BLS reports that employment for environmental scientists is expected to grow by 11 percent through 2026, which is faster than average. Increased public concern about the environment, changing environmental laws and regulations, and the growing demand by businesses for the services of environmental scientists to help minimize the effect their operations have on the environment are projected to spur this growth. Therefore, if you decide to become an environmental scientist, you should be able to land a job that allows you to make a positive impact on the world around you.

Find Out More

California Department of Fish and Wildlife
PO Box 944209
Sacramento, CA 94244
website: www.wildlife.ca.gov

The California Department of Fish and Wildlife helps prevent and rectify environmental problems in the state. It provides information about environmental issues, volunteer opportunities, and interviews with environmental scientists on its website.

EnvironmentalScience.org
website: www.environmentalscience.org

This website promotes environmental science as a field of study. It offers information about environmental science degree programs, scholarships, internships, careers in different environmental specialties, and job postings.

National Institute of Environmental Health Sciences (NIEHS)
PO Box 12233, Mail Drop K3-16
Research Triangle Park, NC 27709
website: www.niehs.nih.gov

The NIEHS is part of the National Institutes of Health. Its mission is to investigate how environmental factors affect human health. It offers a wealth of information about environmental issues, a summer internship program for high school students, and news articles, among other information.

US Environmental Protection Agency (EPA)
1200 Pennsylvania Ave. NW
Washington, DC 20460
website: www.epa.gov

The EPA is a government agency dedicated to protecting the environment. It offers lots of information on its website about all kinds of environmental topics, environmental news, paid and unpaid internships, job postings, a blog, and interviews with environmental scientists.

Epidemiologist

A Few Facts

Number of Jobs
About 6,100 as of 2016

Pay
About $42,810 to $113,560

Educational Requirements
Minimum of a master's degree

Personal Qualities
Detail oriented, good critical-thinking skills

Work Settings
Indoors in offices and laboratories; indoors and outdoors in regions where infection is present

Future Job Outlook
Projected 9 percent job growth through 2026

What Does an Epidemiologist Do?

Do you ever wonder what causes disease outbreaks and other public health issues or what can be done to help prevent or control them? If so, you might like to explore a career as an epidemiologist. Epidemiologists are public health professionals who study the spread, patterns, causes, and effects of diseases and health issues, such as injuries and substance abuse, in an effort to prevent and control them. West Virginia epidemiologist Michael Kilkenny explains, "If we stop watching for those diseases, those diseases will spread, people will get sick and some of those people will die."[18]

These medical investigators use a number of methods to understand, track, and thwart disease outbreaks and the emergence of new illnesses. For example, epidemiologists set up and monitor databases that keep track of disease outbreaks, and they hunt through historical, demographic, and medical data to establish the cause of outbreaks and come up with a plan for how to respond. Epidemiologists also explore and analyze the results of surveys, interviews, and observations of affected individuals and their families, searching for patterns and links between patients and possible risk factors that may influence a disease outbreak. Epidemiologists look at the number of reported cases of an ailment, those affected, and what those affected have in common. They use statistical software to help them analyze this information. In addition, these public health experts perform laboratory tests on samples of tissue, bodily fluids, and bacterial, viral, and fungal cultures. Katrina Roper, a World Health Organization (WHO) epidemiologist, explains, "Our job is to find every single link. We need to find out who infected whom, how, and where."[19]

Epidemiologists present their findings to public health officials, policy makers, and the general public in the form of oral and written reports, as well as in articles in medical journals. Through their work, they reduce the spread of many health threats.

If you decide to become an epidemiologist, you can be a generalist who works on all sorts of public health issues, or you can specialize in one or more areas. These include infectious and/or chronic diseases; maternal, children's, environmental, mental, oral, and/or occupational health; emergency preparedness and response; or substance abuse. Texas epidemiologist Minda Weldon explains,

> Most people know that epidemiologists study outbreaks of infectious diseases but they do a lot more, too. Epidemiologists study cancer, birth defects, exposure to possible environmental toxins, injuries, food poisoning and much more. Some epidemiologists specialize in doing studies to see if new medicines really work.[20]

A Typical Workday

What epidemiologists do on any given workday depends on the cases these experts are investigating and their area of specialization. Much of their time is spent collecting and analyzing statistical data, writing reports, and conducting laboratory experiments and tests. Epidemiologists also might have to travel to regions where a disease outbreak is occurring. There, they gather relevant specimens, observe patients, and conduct interviews and surveys. Epidemiologists may also be involved in educational outreach efforts in local communities. Weldon recollects:

> I spent a lot of time at the computer analyzing data and then writing reports and medical journal articles. I also interviewed people and collected information on surveys. . . . I toured a greenhouse full of poinsettias to try to figure out how workers had been sickened by a pesticide. I went to waste water treatment facilities to get a feel for how much exposure workers had to untreated sewage (a lot!) so that I could design a study to see if workers would benefit from a new vaccine. You see, I was always doing something new.[21]

Education and Training

If this career interests you, you will need a minimum of a master's degree in public health, health statistics, epidemiology, or a related field. Many epidemiologists have a PhD or MD. In preparation for work at the college level, in high school you should take classes in health, biology, chemistry, math, and statistics. Since epidemiologists work with databases, use specialized software, and run computer simulations to evaluate the potential impact of a disease outbreak or other public health issue, computer science classes are useful, too. These classes help hone tech skills. Studying a foreign language is also helpful. Epidemiologists go to locations all over the world and deal with people who speak different languages. Being able to communicate in the predominant language of the region makes this part of the job easier.

In college, aspiring epidemiologists can choose among different majors, but many graduate programs prefer candidates who have a strong foundation in health science, biology, research methods, and statistics. Graduate course work includes classes in statistics, biochemistry, physiology, psychology, immunology, and public health. In addition, graduate students are usually involved in research projects and in many cases are expected to produce a thesis based on their research. Says Weldon,

> I studied lots of different things including biology, chemistry, and lots of statistics. I also worked closely with a professor to do a research study about how different diseases affect the ability of older people to live independently.[22]

Many prospective epidemiologists get practical experience by doing an internship or volunteering with a public health organization. The Centers for Disease Control and Prevention (CDC), many state and local public health departments, and charitable health organizations provide opportunities for students to volunteer or to work as interns and in summer jobs. These positions allow students to explore what it is like to be an epidemiologist and apply their learning to real-life situations.

Skills and Personality

If you become an epidemiologist, not only do you need to be knowledgeable about diseases, public health, and the human body, you should have great research and organizational skills and enjoy working with and analyzing statistical data. As an epidemiologist, it's important to be detail oriented and have excellent critical-thinking skills. These skills ensure that epidemiologists catch the tiny—but important—clues needed to draw logical conclusions about how best to respond to disease outbreaks.

In addition, you can't be squeamish. Epidemiologists observe and interview people with communicable diseases, and they work with blood and other bodily fluids. In such situations, epidemiologists wear protective gear.

Respect for other cultures is also essential. Disease outbreaks occur all over the world. Epidemiologists are often sent to foreign countries, where they interview subjects and work with people with diverse backgrounds. In order to gain their subjects' trust and work as an effective team with foreign colleagues, epidemiologists must be sensitive to and tolerant of different cultural values. Being able to speak the native language helps in these instances, too. Therefore, having an aptitude for learning other languages is a plus. In addition, since epidemiologists often work as a team with other epidemiologists and health care professionals, if you pursue a job in this field, you should be able to work with and get along with others.

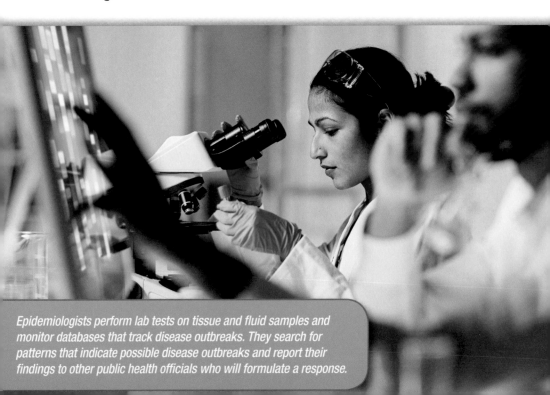

Epidemiologists perform lab tests on tissue and fluid samples and monitor databases that track disease outbreaks. They search for patterns that indicate possible disease outbreaks and report their findings to other public health officials who will formulate a response.

Working Conditions

Most epidemiologists work a traditional five-day, forty-hour work-week. However, they may work longer hours during public health emergencies. These public health heroes work in clean, well-lit offices and laboratories, as well as in clinical settings like field hospitals and in developing regions that may lack electricity or indoor plumbing. These regions may have limited access to high-tech medical resources and technology. The work of epidemiologists can also be challenging in locations that lack established systems for collecting health-related data.

When working out in the field, in clinical settings, and in laboratories, these professionals risk being exposed to infectious diseases. To shield themselves, epidemiologists wear protective gear such as gloves, masks, and sometimes even hazmat suits while conducting experiments, and they follow strict protocols out in the field. For instance, in order to avoid direct contact with contagious individuals, during a 2014 outbreak of the Ebola virus in Sierra Leone, CDC epidemiologists conducted interviews with patients through a window. One of these epidemiologists, John Redd, recalls,

> The most important thing was no touching. No shaking hands, no hugging. . . . It was really something to live in that reality where you never touch another person. . . . Also, before being posted, we were trained at CDC in Atlanta in the use of personal protective equipment which all of us carried in backpacks at all times.[23]

Employers and Pay

As an epidemiologist, you'll probably be employed by a state or local government or by a federal or international public health agency like the CDC or WHO. You might also be employed by a hospital, college or university, or scientific research service. Some epidemiologists work for pharmaceutical companies.

According to the Bureau of Labor Statistics (BLS), as of May 2017 the median annual salary for epidemiologists was $69,660. The lowest-paid 10 percent earned less than $42,810, while the top-paid 10 percent earned more than $113,560. In addition to their salary, most epidemiologists receive employee benefits that include paid sick and vacation days, health insurance, and a retirement plan.

What Is the Future Outlook for Epidemiologists?

The BLS reports that employment for epidemiologists is expected to grow by 9 percent through 2026, which is about as fast as the average for all occupations. Employment opportunities should be greatest in local and state health agencies and in hospitals. Although candidates face competition in landing their dream jobs, it may be well worth the effort. In fact, in its annual ranking of careers, *U.S. World & News Report* ranks epidemiology as 2018's best science career. That's not surprising, since epidemiologists save many lives.

Find Out More

Career Village
1003 Clark Way
Palo Alto, CA 94304
website: www.careervillage.org

Career Village is an organization that provides information on career topics and specific careers, including epidemiology. The website matches career questions from students all over the world with thousands of experienced professionals in relevant career fields.

Centers for Disease Control and Prevention (CDC)
1600 Clifton Rd. NE
Atlanta, GA 30329
website: www.cdc.gov

The CDC is part of the US Department of Health and Human Services. Its job is to protect the public from diseases and other public health threats. Its website is packed with articles and information about public health issues. It also provides information and videos about careers in epidemiology, information about summer jobs and internships, and job postings.

Public Health Online
website: www.publichealthonline.org

Public Health Online is a website that provides information about public health careers for students and other interested individuals. It includes specific information about a career as an epidemiologist, articles, and information about college programs, scholarships, and grants.

World Health Organization (WHO)
Avenue Appia 20
1202 Geneva, Switzerland
website: www.who.int

WHO is an international organization, with offices throughout the world, dedicated to protecting public health. Its website provides a wealth of information about specific diseases, disease outbreaks, and how epidemiologists respond. The website also provides interviews with epidemiologists working in the field.

Fire Investigator

What Does a Fire Investigator Do?

If you love solving mysteries and don't mind getting dirty, you might be interested in exploring a career as a fire investigator. Fire investigators determine the origin and cause of fires and fire-related explosions, including whether or not a fire is caused by arson or negligence.

After a fire occurs, fire investigators explore the scene of the fire. They look for things like frayed wires or the presence of accelerants that might have increased the strength and spread of the blaze. Investigators also look for heat-related damage patterns (burn patterns), which help them understand how the fire spread. These experts comb through layers and layers of ash and charred debris looking for evidence of the cause and origin of the fire. Collecting samples from the scene for laboratory analysis, which might reveal fingerprints, the presence of accelerants, or other evidence of arson, is another part of the job. Other duties include taking photos and making diagrams of the scene. And fire investigators interview witnesses and firefighters to find out what they may know about the fire. Ron Humphrey, an Iowa fire investigator, explains, "We look for things like the burn patterns, multiple points of origin, witnesses who might have seen something. We try to keep all options in play so we can cover all bases to determine the cause of a fire."[24]

Once they've gathered all of the needed information and samples at the scene, investigators and others analyze everything. Based on that analysis, the investigators come up with a theory about the fire's cause, origin, and spread. This scenario may be tested by re-creating the fire in a controlled environment. Lee Miller, a British fire investigator, explains:

> Every investigation is carried out using the scientific method. Basically we gather all the information and data that can help us come up with a hypothesis—a theory on how the fire started. . . . Once we have the relevant information, we analyze it and develop a number of theories on how it started. Each theory is then tested against the information we have until, ideally, we have only one credible cause left.[25]

Also known as arson investigators or fire marshals, these professionals are part detective, part fire scientist, and part law enforcer. A fire investigator quite literally sifts through ashes looking for clues. He or she must know about flammable materials and how fires spread. And investigators make sure that people who start fires or don't follow fire safety codes are held accountable. These experts also keep detailed records of every case and often are required to testify in legal proceedings related to a fire. Some fire investigators also serve as fire inspectors, a job that entails inspecting buildings to ensure they meet fire codes.

A Typical Workday

Fire investigators are busy people. According to the US Fire Administration, on average, about 1 million fires result in more than three thousand deaths each year in the United States. "This isn't a job for a lazy man,"[26] says Paul Horgan, a Massachusetts state trooper who works closely with the Office of the State Fire Marshal. Indeed, if you decide to become a fire investigator, you probably won't be bored. Every day is different, and you don't always know what to expect.

Some days are spent out in the field interviewing witnesses and exploring the scene of a recent fire. Such exploration requires great care so that any possible evidence is not destroyed or contaminated. "Scene preservation is of paramount importance at an arson incident,"[27] Miller explains. Fire investigators use a small trowel and a brush to sift through the ashes, searching for evidence such as charred wood, glass shards, metal fragments, and bits of rags with accelerant residue, which they collect and carefully package. They also rely on a camera and their photography skills to take pictures of the scene.

Once they are back in the office, investigators study these pictures, looking for clues to the fire's origin and cause. In fact, there are some days in which fire investigators spend all of their time in the office poring over photographs, diagrams, written observations, and witness interviews in hopes of uncovering relevant information. Analyzing samples, studying laboratory test results, documenting their findings, and writing reports also fills their time. Meeting and consulting with other professionals such as chemists, police, and crime scene investigators is another aspect of the job. Other days are spent in courtrooms, providing expert testimony in trials of fire-related cases.

Education and Training

Fire investigators need at least a high school diploma, as well as knowledge about fires and crime scene investigations. Most fire investigators gain that experience in law enforcement or as professional firefighters. One good way for you to prepare for this career is to do community service at your local fire department or become a volunteer firefighter. Both experiences will help you learn more about what fire investigators do. Taking a chemistry class in high school is also helpful. Knowledge of chemistry helps fire investigators understand the properties of different chemicals

A Team Effort

"Just got to participate in a fatal fire investigation last week. The teamwork was great. There were several of us from different agencies. It was a true collaborative effort, as there were firefighters, fire investigators, detectives, and CSIs [crime scene investigators]. It's always good to take part in these, as you learn from others in a real life scenario."

—Robert Rullen, fire investigator, San Francisco Bay Area

Robert Rullen, "Fatal Fire," *Fire for Effect* (blog), September 6, 2009. https://fire4fx.word press.com.

and how heat affects them. It also helps prepare you for postsecondary applied chemistry classes.

Although some fire departments hire individuals straight out of high school, studying fire science at a community college will help you prepare for this career. Rookie investigators also receive on-the-job-training. Many candidates pursue a one- or two-year certification program offered by many community colleges. Individuals who successfully complete the two-year program can also earn an associate's degree. Course work includes classes in applied chemistry, fire analysis, legal procedures, fire-related human behavior, and evidence gathering. Fire science programs prepare aspiring fire investigators to successfully complete a certification exam based on industry standards established by the National Fire Protection Association. Although certification is voluntary, being certified identifies individuals as fire science experts and, for that reason, may give you a leg up in getting a job and advancing in your career.

Skills and Personality

Being a fire investigator is a complex job with lots of responsibility. To solve fire cases, these men and women need technical knowledge and training, as well as nontechnical skills. Technical knowledge

A fire investigator inspects the likely origin location of a 2017 fire in the Angeles National Forest. Whether a fire occurs in a forest or a house or business, investigators carefully examine the scene to learn how the fire started and how it spread.

includes an understanding of fire dynamics, building construction and materials, electricity, and chemistry. Robert Duval, a senior fire investigator with the National Fire Protection Association, explains:

> You are looking at something that was destroyed and you have to be able to put it back together again either in your mind or physically to determine the origin and cause. Technical training plays a role in determining a lot of the factors in terms of fire behavior and how it attacked the structure you are looking at, whether it be an appliance, piece of equipment, or building.[28]

In addition to technical knowledge, if this is your career path you'll also need to be physically fit since combing through fire scenes requires frequent bending, crouching, and lifting of debris. Fire investigators also must be meticulous. Attention to even the tiniest detail is required; otherwise it would be easy to miss a small but important clue. Having a logical mind and being an excellent problem solver are other vital abilities. As a fire investigator, you must be able to analyze evidence from a fire and come up with a logical conclusion based on carefully assembled facts. "You have to be conscientious and have a mind that likes to figure things out. You really can't take shortcuts,"[29] Horgan explains.

These professionals also must be able to work well with others. They often team up with firefighters, law enforcement personnel, chemists, and engineers in order to solve fire mysteries. Having good people skills also helps fire investigators in interviewing witnesses, as does being a good listener. Good listeners let witnesses tell their story without interrupting. This helps witnesses feel more comfortable and therefore more likely to reveal more information.

Working Conditions

Fire investigators work in offices and at fire scenes. Most work full time. Since fires can happen at any time, and fire scenes must be investigated promptly, before evidence can be lost or contaminated, fire investigators may be called in to work nights, holidays, and weekends. While working in the field, they risk burns from still-hot debris, electric shock, and injury from falling objects, and they may be exposed to health risks related to poor ventilation, smoke inhalation, and the lingering presence of hazardous materials and gases. To reduce their risk, investigators exercise

Do You Have What It Takes?

"If you can interview well and learn to read people, and mix that with diagramming, investigation, photography, and report writing, you will be a good fire investigator."

—Paul Zipper, fire investigator, Office of the State Fire Marshal, Massachusetts

Quoted in Genevieve Belfiglio, "How to Become a Fire Investigator," Inter Fire Online, 2019. www.interfire.org.

caution as they move through fire scenes. And they wear protective gear, such as special boots, overalls, gloves, helmets, filter masks, and self-contained breathing devices.

Employers and Pay

If you become a fire investigator, you'll probably be employed by a state department of fire safety or a city or county fire department. Some fire investigators are employed by insurance firms or companies that provide investigation and security services. They are also employed by the US Fire Administration and the Bureau of Alcohol, Tobacco, Firearms and Explosives.

The Bureau of Labor Statistics (BLS) reports that as of May 2017 the median annual salary for fire investigators was $59,260. The lowest-paid 10 percent earned less than $34,800, while the top-paid 10 percent earned more than $95,960. In addition to their salary, most fire investigators receive employee benefits that include paid sick and vacation days, health insurance, and a retirement plan.

What Is the Future Outlook for Fire Investigators?

The BLS predicts that employment opportunities for fire investigators and inspectors will grow by 7 percent from 2016 to 2026. This growth is about as fast as the average for all professions. You may face stiff competition for available positions. Opportunities should be greatest for candidates who have completed some fire science education and have firefighting or crime scene investigation training.

Find Out More

FireScience.org
website: www.firescience.org

FireScience.org is a website that provides information about careers in fire science, including fire investigator. It offers lists of certification, degree, and training programs; articles; a blog; and advice from experts.

Inter Fire Online
website: www.interfire.org

This website serves as a resource for fire investigators and other fire science professionals. It has lots of articles about fire investigating, fire safety, and fire science. It also offers videos, online training classes, certification information, and other resources.

National Association of Fire Investigators (NAFI)
4900 Manatee Ave. W., Suite 104
Bradenton, FL 34209
website: www.nafi.org

The NAFI is an association made up of fire science professionals. It is dedicated to increasing the knowledge and skills of individuals involved in fire investigation. It offers training programs, job postings, publications, articles, and conferences and administers certification exams.

US Fire Administration
16825 S. Seton Ave.
Emmitsburg, MD 21727
website: www.usfa.fema.gov

The US Fire Administration is a government agency concerned with fire prevention. It offers lots of online and face-to-face training and classes for fire professionals, publications, job postings, and plenty of information about fire science and fire safety.

Forensic Accountant

A Few Facts

Number of Jobs
About 1.4 million
as of 2016*

Pay
About $45,220 to
$104,441

Educational Requirements
Bachelor's degree

Personal Qualities
Ethical,
mathematical,
detail oriented

Work Settings
Indoors in an office
setting

Future Job Outlook
Projected 10
percent job growth
through 2026*

* This number is for
accountants and auditors,
which includes forensic
accountants

What Does a Forensic Accountant Do?

Forensic accountants are sleuths who gather, review, investigate, and analyze paper and electronic records for evidence of crimes and irregularities involving, but not limited to, embezzlement, fraud, money laundering, tax evasion, counterfeiting, identity theft, and civil financial disputes. According to journalist Justin Pope, they "inhabit a cloak and dagger corner of the accounting world. Their job: respond at a moment's notice when a client spots trouble—anything from . . . fraud to a top executive cooking the books to industrial espionage."[30]

These men and women are responsible for putting many criminals behind bars. For example, forensic accountants helped investigators working on the case against Paul Manafort, a political consultant and former campaign advisor to several Republican presidents, including Donald Trump. In 2018 Manafort was convicted of eight counts of tax and bank fraud. Writer Richard Singer explains, "When it comes to fraud, there is no asset more valuable than the forensic accountant.

. . . While accounting may not seem like a traditionally exciting job, forensic accountants have the ability to investigate serious crime, working hand in hand with the legal system. What could be more exciting than that?"[31]

To do their job, these number-crunching investigators gather, pore over, and analyze all sorts of financial records and related material to search for financial wrongdoings, determine the net worth of a business or individual, trace funds, or discover hidden assets. By following the money trail, forensic accountants are usually able to identify not only financial wrongdoings but also the people involved. In fact, they often interview suspects in order to gather information. Juan Roman, an accounting professor at St. Leo University, a Florida college, explains, "They look beyond the numbers to learn the specifics. They search all records, emails, bank statements and journals. They interview the accused and they trace assets."[32]

Forensic accountants present their findings in the form of written reports and visual aids, which may be used as evidence in trials. They may also write questions for attorneys to ask witnesses concerning financial matters. Forensic accountants' knowledge of the law and legal proceedings helps set them apart from other certified public accountants (CPAs). Indeed, although most forensic accountants are CPAs, most CPAs do not engage in financial sleuthing.

A Typical Workday

Forensic accountants do not have a set routine. What they do on any given day depends on their employer and the cases they are working on. Australian forensic accountant Fiona Pang says:

> The best thing is that every day involves something different. Throughout the year you get the opportunity to work on numerous matters in a variety of different industries so there are always new challenges. The matters I have been involved in often get you thinking about the issues, planning how to solve the problem and then taking into consideration how the work should be undertaken . . . so it can be an interesting challenge.[33]

Some days are spent investigating without necessarily knowing what misdeeds, if any, have occurred. This involves searching through and analyzing years and years of financial records and gathering and studying emails, telephone records, and other communications in search of evidence related to monetary transactions. According to Indiana forensic accountant Susan Brackney, this aspect of the work is like "putting together a jigsaw puzzle when you haven't seen the picture."[34]

Translating the results of their analysis into written reports that nonaccountants can also understand fills much of the forensic accountant's time. Other duties include meetings with clients, attorneys, law enforcement personnel, and sometimes even individuals who are suspected of having involvement in financial crimes. Some days are spent in a courtroom, presenting evidence that is vital to determining the amount of financial damages to be paid to wronged parties and/or the guilt or innocence of defendants.

Education and Training

If you decide to become a forensic accountant, you'll need a bachelor's degree of approximately 150 credit hours and a CPA license. Most candidates major in accounting, finance, or a related field. Accounting classes require solid math skills. You can prepare for challenging college course work by taking math classes in high school. High school computer classes, too, are helpful since they prepare you to work with databases, spreadsheets, and financial software. And because forensic accountants must be able to write and speak well, developing these skills through drama and journalism classes is also useful.

College courses you'll be required to take include accounting principles, finance, economics, auditing methods, taxation law, ethics, and fraud investigation. Many aspiring forensic accountants also take classes in criminal justice and financial management.

After completing college and often a year of required work experience, candidates take the Uniform Certified Public Accountant

No Typical Day

"It is difficult to define a typical day as a forensic accountant as much of my activity is determined by the details of whichever case or cases I'm busy with. Most of my time is spent either analyzing facts and data or preparing reports and presentations in relation to the analyses I've completed. . . . The cases I've been involved with have ranged from multi-million dollar fraud investigations to preparing business valuations in the context of damages assessments in support of high profile litigation matters."

—Boyd Harris, forensic accountant, senior manager at Axiom Forensics, Sydney, Australia

Quoted in David Mullins, "A Day in the Life of a Forensic Accountant," Axiom Forensics, June 11, 2015. https://axiomforensics.com.

exam, which allows them to work as and hold the title of a certified public accountant. Although it is not required, many also obtain certification as a certified fraud examiner and/or forensic certified public accountant, which indicates that they are experts in forensic accounting.

Skills and Personality

Forensic accountants must excel at sorting and searching through large amounts of information, identifying patterns, and assessing the meaning or importance of that information. Often these abilities develop only with experience. Andrew P. Ross, a CPA, certified fraud examiner, and partner in a large New York accounting firm, explains,

I would tell accounting students that this field is a great field to get into; however, experience in the accounting field and obtaining a base of knowledge are important before jumping into forensic accounting. Having a solid, basic knowledge of certain accounting concepts can greatly assist in your career.[35]

More than Numbers

"The numbers are the numbers are the numbers. It's how you get behind those numbers and how you're trained to look at those numbers and what really made those up. How is this occurring and why is this occurring becomes very, very important."

—Darryl Neier, forensic accountant

Quoted in Greg S. Saitz, "My Turn: Forensic Accountant Darryl Neier," NJ.com, March 25, 2008. www.nj.com.

In addition, these financial researchers must be knowledgeable about legal concepts and procedures, including understanding the rights of individuals under investigation and the rules involving evidence. They also must be meticulous investigators that pay keen attention to detail so that they do not miss any clues. Being curious and persistent are also essential since these professionals often have to search through lots of information over and over again in order to identify financial crimes.

If you enter this field, you should have good written and oral communication skills, too, so that you can write reports and provide clear, concise testimony in court. Integrity and discretion are other vital traits. Forensic accountants are held to high ethical standards. These experts are privy to all kinds of financial and personal information; divulging this information, unless mandated by law, can cause harm to individuals and businesses. Another part of acting ethically is being objective and unbiased. Forensic accountants must handle each case with an open mind and not let preconceived notions about a suspect's guilt or innocence taint the investigation. According to Heinz E. Ickert, a forensic accountant practicing in Ohio and Florida:

The forensic accountant must not only begin the engagement with an open mind considering all options and theories, he must remain so during the course of the assignment. The unbiased forensic accountant will consider all evidence uncovered, including that which does not support the currently held most plausible theory of the case. Being truly objective means being willing to put aside old theories and suspicions and consider new evidence as it presents itself.[36]

Working Conditions

Forensic accountants work in an office setting, except when traveling to their clients' places of business. Appearances in court as expert witnesses also take forensic accountants away from their office. Most forensic accountants work a traditional five-day, forty-hour workweek. They spend much of their time seated in front of a computer. Depending on their employer and the importance of the case, forensic accountants may work independently or as part of a team.

Employers and Pay

Forensic accountants may work in either the private or public sector. They work for accounting firms, insurance companies, law firms, and consulting firms that provide accounting services. Forensic accountants are also employed by the military, local and state law enforcement agencies, and federal agencies like the FBI, Naval Criminal Investigative Service, and the Internal Revenue Service. Opportunities also exist abroad. Some forensic accountants are self-employed; they work as consultants for businesses and individuals who require their services.

If you decide to become a forensic accountant, you should earn a comfortable living. According to PayScale, a website that gives salary information for various professions, as of 2019, forensic accountants earned an average annual salary of $65,542, ranging from about $45,220 to $104,441. In addition, PayScale reports that these professionals often receive annual bonuses ranging from $779 to $15,024 and profit sharing ranging from $978 to $8,000. Unless they are self-employed, most forensic accountants also receive benefits, including health insurance, paid sick and vacation leave, and retirement plans.

What Is the Future Outlook for Forensic Accountants?

The Bureau of Labor Statistics does not collect data specifically about forensic accountants, but rather includes them with all accountants and auditors. It predicts that employment opportunities for all types of accountants and auditors will grow by 10 percent from 2016 to 2026. This is faster than average for all professions.

Many accounting, law, and other firms are adding forensic accountants to their rosters in response to social and technological changes. According to Ross:

> For one thing, society today is much more litigious, creating an increased need for forensic accountants. Over the years, attorneys who litigate cases have become more knowledgeable about the advantages of hiring a forensic accountant in certain matters. In addition, today's technology has made financial crimes much more difficult to identify, leading to a greater need for the forensic accountant.[37]

So, if this career suits you, there should be a job for you.

Find Out More

Forensic Accounting
website: https://forensic-accountant.weebly.com

This Canadian website provides lots of information about forensic accounting, including what forensic accountants do, their daily tasks and functions, required education, skills and personality requirements, and future outlook for the job.

Forensic CPA Society
PO Box 31060
Spokane, WA 99223
website: www.fcpas.org

This organization consists of forensic certified public accountants. It provides information about this career on its website, news articles related to forensic accounting, a forensic accountant finder tool, and information about obtaining certification, including study guides.

International Institute of Certified Forensic Accountants (IICFA)

8 The Green, Suite A
Dover, DE 19901
website: http://iicfaglobal.com

The IICFA is an international organization composed of forensic accountants and forensic accounting students. It is dedicated to promoting forensic accounting education. It provides information about certification, education and training, global job postings, interviews with forensic accountants, and e-learning opportunities.

National Association of Forensic Accountants (NAFA)

10001 W. Oakland Park Blvd., Suite 301
Sunrise, FL 33351
website: www.nafanet.com

NAFA provides certification and training opportunities for accountants who want to specialize in forensic accounting. On its website, this organization offers information about the history of forensic accounting, what forensic accounting involves, and the different types of cases related to forensic accounting.

Geological and Petroleum Technician

A Few Facts

Number of Jobs
About 15,000 as of 2016

Pay
About $27,010 to $108,420

Educational Requirements
Minimum of an associate's degree

Personal Qualities
Physical stamina, analytic skills

Work Settings
Indoors in laboratories and offices; outdoors in the field

Future Job Outlook
Projected 16 percent job growth through 2026

What Does a Geological and Petroleum Technician Do?

If you enjoy studying rocks and minerals, working with your hands, and using complex tools and equipment, you might consider a career as a geological and petroleum technician. Geological and petroleum technicians assist geologists and engineers in exploring and identifying the location and characteristics of oil, gas, and mineral deposits and in extracting these natural resources. Using ground-penetrating radar, sophisticated drilling and seismic equipment, and other tools, these technicians collect samples of soil, rocks, and minerals from selected sites. They examine and analyze the samples for evidence of oil and other hydrocarbons, valuable ores, and precious metals. Technicians also study and analyze the strength of rock samples to determine whether a mine can be safely constructed on a particular site.

Once they have completed their analysis, these geological professionals present their findings in written reports, charts and graphs, and two- and three-dimensional surface and subsurface maps, created with the help of a geographic information system (GIS) and other specialized software. Oil and mining companies use this information to decide whether drilling or mining a site is safe, practical, and financially reasonable.

Another part of the technician's job is evaluating existing mines, oil fields, and drilling equipment for safety and efficiency. If technicians see problems, they work with engineers to come up with solutions. Dan Carrocci, a Canadian geological technician who started his own mining exploration and drilling business, explains, "What I love is that it's challenging. Nothing is easy, you have to wear many hats. You have to be a mechanic, a geologist, a weatherman, and a little bit of everything."[38]

Geological and petroleum technicians can focus on just field or just laboratory work or can be generalists who do both field and laboratory work. They can also choose to work in a specific type of mining or in the oil and gas industry, or they can opt to work in all types of mining and extraction. For example, Paddy Campbell is a geological technician who specializes in laboratory work. He works for a gold mining company in Ireland. Campbell explains,

> I am part of the geology team that works on the drill core [a small core of rock withdrawn from bedrock] after it comes in from the exploration site. We are responsible for identifying areas of strength and weakness in the rock to enable the mine engineers to design a mine that will operate to the highest safety standards.[39]

A Typical Workday

What geological and petroleum technicians do during a typical workday depends on their employer and whether they are working in the office or in the field. In the field, technicians gather samples of rock, minerals, crude oil, and soil from different depths. They use specialized drills and seismic instruments to extract samples from bedrock. The samples are taken to laboratories or offices, where technicians study the samples under a microscope and perform a variety of tests on the samples in order to determine their chemical and physical content and characteristics. Technicians record their findings in written reports, as well as maps and graphic representations, that identify which areas and depths contain resources. Canadian geological and petroleum technician Steve Livie explains,

> We're actively drilling, doing core analyses, taking porosity, permeability, fluid saturations, washing the samples, getting the samples back here [the laboratory] for analysis. [We] put this all together. It's presented in . . . a graphic representation of all the parameters, all the engineering."[40]

In addition, these professionals may spend some of their workday installing and maintaining field and laboratory equipment.

Education and Training

Geological and petroleum technicians need at least an associate's degree in geological technology, mining technology, petroleum science, applied science, or a related field. This takes about two years and is offered at many community colleges and technical institutes. You can start preparing for this career and for postsecondary course work in high school by taking earth science and chemistry

Safety and Accuracy

"We have to work to strict standards and always carry out quality assurance and control checks as part of our job. This ensures the company can build an accurate model of where the gold is found and the best and safest way to mine it."

—Paddy Campbell, geological technician, Dalradian Gold, Northern Ireland

Paddy Campbell, "A Day in the Life at Dalradian," *Ulster Herald* (Omagh, Northern Ireland), July 6, 2018. https://ulsterherald.com.

classes. Clearly, you need a strong background in earth science to do this job. You should also be knowledgeable in chemistry to analyze and understand the chemical composition of rock samples.

Since this job requires individuals to use complex software, computer science classes are also useful. So are language arts classes. David McManus, a geological technology instructor at Northlands College in Saskatchewan, Canada, explains, "Geotechs have to write. They have to prepare reports. So, good writing skills are very important."[41]

Postsecondary course work focuses on geology, chemistry, physics, and industry-specific math. Students also receive instruction in oil exploration and mine and oil field safety. Most classes are hands-on. Students practice operating simulated and real drilling equipment; gathering and analyzing soil, rock, and mineral samples; and using GIS and other industry-specific software. The training is aimed at helping students develop practical skills so that upon graduation they can go right to work with a minimum of on-the-job training.

Skills and Personality

If you are interested in this career, you should enjoy working with machinery, scientific instruments, and computers. You should also have good eyesight and eye-hand coordination, which will enable you to operate drilling and other equipment and to prepare and study samples. Being physically fit is essential, too. Fieldwork involves physical labor that requires muscular strength, as well as fine motor coordination. And because working in and around mines and oil fields can be dangerous, if you enter this field, you must be the type of person who makes safety a priority.

Being detail oriented is another valuable characteristic. Geological and petroleum technicians must be accurate. Misidentifying the location of oil or ores can be quite costly. Plus, even a small error in assessing the strength of rock at a prospective mine site can lead to a disaster that costs lives and wreaks lasting environmental damage. Indeed, to ensure accuracy, technicians double-check or even triple-check their results.

In addition, these professionals work both as part of a team and independently. So if you pursue this career, you should be dependable and able to work on your own with minimal supervision. At the same time, you must be able to work well with others.

Working Conditions

Geological and petroleum technicians work under diverse conditions. Technicians work outdoors a lot, in good and bad weather. And although some mines and drill sites are located near established communities, many are located in remote areas, including offshore. Technicians rely on a wide variety of transport in order to get to remote sites. Crystal Smith, a geological technology student, spent a summer working in the field as part of her training. She recalls, "Exploring by helicopter was hands-down the most exciting thing I did all summer. My field supervisor allowed me to navigate to a site using a GPS . . . and the best part of it all was flying around with the door open."[42]

Laboratory specialists may work in company offices and laboratories located in towns or cities, putting in a standard five-day workweek. Sometimes, though, laboratory technicians may work at remote sites. In fact, in many cases laboratories and offices are housed in makeshift buildings near drilling and mining sites. On-site work schedules can be long and irregular due to changing weather conditions. Technicians are often required to stay in the field collecting and analyzing samples and monitoring equipment for many days, then are off for an equal amount of time. Livie explains, "I work anywhere between ten days and two weeks. In between . . . when you do have time off, you have some good time off. You pack your gear, you go home for a week or so, and then you come back and do it all over."[43]

Safety is a major concern for technicians working near drill sites and mines. Falls and accidents are not uncommon. Moreover, blowouts may occur if an oil well's pressure is not properly controlled. At mining sites, rock slides and cave-ins are always possible, regardless of how careful the workers are. To protect themselves while out in the field, geological and petroleum technicians observe strict safety rules and wear protective garments such as safety glasses, hard hats, and steel-toe boots. They might also wear respirators if there is a chance of exposure to coal dust, for example.

Employers and Pay

If you pursue this career, you'll probably be employed by an oil and gas extraction company, a mining company, or an organization that provides engineering, management, or technical consulting services. Your job location could be almost anywhere in the world. According to the Bureau of Labor Statistics (BLS), the median annual salary for geological and petroleum technicians was $54,190 as of 2017. The lowest-paid 10 percent earned less than $27,010, and the highest-paid 10 percent earned more than $108,420. Technicians also usually receive health and accident insurance, paid sick and vacation days, and profit sharing.

What Is the Future Outlook for Geological and Petroleum Technicians?

The BLS predicts that employment opportunities for geological and petroleum technicians will grow by 16 percent from 2016 to

2026, which is faster than average. Growth is largely dependent on the demand for oil, gas, and minerals, which is expected to continue at the current pace or increase. Opportunities should be greatest if you have strong technical and analytical abilities.

Find Out More

EnvironmentalScience.org
website: www.environmentalscience.org

EnvironmentalScience.org is an organization that promotes environmental science education and careers. It offers information about different environmental careers, including geological and petroleum technician.

Nevada Mining Association
201 W. Liberty St., Suite 300
Reno, Nevada 89501
website: www.nevadamining.org

This association promotes Nevada's mining industry. It provides information about different mining careers, including geological technician; information about mining; and interviews with people in related fields on its website.

Study.com
website: https://study.com

This website helps people learn about different careers, including a career as a geological technician. It offers information about the job, required education and training, and wages.

Work BC
website: www.workbc.ca

Work BC is an official website of the Canadian province of British Columbia, dedicated to helping people find jobs in the province. It provides information about many different careers, including geological and petroleum technician, as well as an interview with a geotech, job postings, and information about education and training.

Information Security Analyst

What Does an Information Security Analyst Do?

One of the greatest threats to individuals, businesses, government agencies, and other organizations are cyberattacks. Without being physically present, hackers can steal or corrupt confidential data and disable computer systems and networks. They can cause businesses to lose large sums of money; disrupt power grids, energy pipelines, and transportation and drinking water systems; interfere with military operations; and compromise national security.

If you would like to help prevent cyberattacks, are fascinated with information technology, and can't resist a challenge, you might consider a career as an information security analyst. Information security analysts, also known as cybersecurity analysts, cyberanalysts, or security analysts, protect computer systems and networks from viruses and malicious hackers. Using specialized software, they monitor, study, and analyze computer systems and networks, searching for vulnerabilities and suspicious activity.

To identify a computer system's weaknesses and strengths, information security analysts conduct penetration tests. In these tests, information security analysts try to both break into and thwart an attack on the system. "It's like you are arguing with yourself," says California cybersecurity expert Vijay Upadhyaya. "You are an attacker or thinking like one and then next minute you are a defender and trying to stop that attack."[44]

Once the test is complete, these cyberprofessionals analyze the results, noting which parts of the system are weak, which defenses worked, and which attacks, if any, the test defeated. If the security experts detect any weaknesses, they institute measures to fix vulnerable areas. These measures can involve writing code or installing hardware that strengthens the network's firewall. Australian information security analyst Alexis Coupe explains,

When hackers decide to steal confidential documents, they try to make sure that they are not detected by the security team so they can come back in the future. We try and get ahead in the game by simulating those activities and then trying to detect it ourselves.[45]

In addition to looking for and plugging up system weaknesses, cyberanalysts relentlessly analyze bits and bytes of network traffic in search of suspicious activity. According to Colorado information security analyst Jim Treinen, they focus on asking questions that can be used to anticipate trouble: "What are the key activities on the network? What [activity] are we monitoring? Is there something that we see that is a potential risk that we need to really come up to speed on quickly?"[46]

If security analysts discover any suspicious activity, they take steps to block it. But despite their best efforts, some cyberattacks make it through. When an attack occurs, these men and women defend the network by cutting off digital roadways and setting traps within the network to confuse, block, or intercept attackers. Plus, security analysts gather and analyze digital evidence, which they use to figure out how the hackers got into the system and possibly to identify the culprits. They document the results of their research and actions in logs and written reports. In addition,

One Information Security Expert's Career Path

"Early in my career, I was working for a computer company when someone stole the source code for our software. The company formed an information security team and developed a tool to identify when systems were misconfigured or when they were broken into. I had been teaching people how to use software and computers, so I taught people how to work the security tool. After that, I became the security guru for the computer room. And since then, I've done everything and anything when it comes to [information technology] security."

—Candy Alexander, New Hampshire cybersecurity consultant

Quoted in Elka Torpey, "Interview with a Cybersecurity Consultant," Bureau of Labor Statistics, Career Outlook, January 2018. www.bls.gov.

these experts are involved in creating cybersecurity-related plans and procedures, training staff to follow these procedures, and monitoring their compliance.

A Typical Workday

There is no typical workday for these men and women. Everything depends on what's occurring on the network. "We never know what is going to happen," Treinen says. "A day can start out calm or start out on fire and very quickly go from one or another."[47]

On a quiet day, information security analysts can be found seated in front of a computer, scanning company computers for viruses and malware, monitoring network traffic, performing penetration tests, and updating systems. They also spend quiet time checking on whether cybersafety procedures are being followed, logging their findings, writing reports, attending meetings, and training staff members on security practices. Coupe explains,

Through constant monitoring and analysis of the network, we seek to detect the theft of sensitive information, spreading of malware, phishing campaigns, and the occasional network intrusion. That being said, it's not like CSI (crime scene investigation): it's 80 per cent cyber analysis and 20 per cent excitement![48]

However, when a threat is perceived, things change drastically. These cyberwarriors go into battle mode, analyzing the threat and coming up with creative ways to counter it and clean up the damage.

Education and Training

Information security analysts need a bachelor's degree in computer science, information technology, cybersecurity, or a related field. If this career interests you, you can start gaining the skills you'll need by taking computer science classes in high school. Cybersecurity analysts must have stellar technical skills. They need to be adept at using different operating systems, software, and programming languages. Plus, analysts should be able to write code and program, and they should have an expert understanding of how computer systems and networks function, as well as the hardware involved. Although high school computer science classes won't give you all these skills, the classes should provide you with a strong foundation that will prepare you for the rigors of college study.

Language arts and speech classes, which are required in most high schools, will help you develop communication skills

A Hot Field

"We're hiring like mad. . . . We don't have the workforce right now to challenge the problem efficiently. We're in a bit of a scramble mode to help get caught up and train folks to get our arms around a big national challenge."

—Scott Cramer, director of the cybersecurity program at Idaho National Laboratory

Quoted in Keith Ridler, "Idaho Lab Protects US Infrastructure from Cyber Attacks," *Forensic Magazine*, January 2, 2019. www.forensicmag.com.

that will come in handy. Information security analysts write reports and policies, train other employees on security issues, and meet with upper management to discuss security matters. They have to be able to communicate all this information accurately and in a way that everyone can understand, which requires good writing and speaking skills.

In college, aspiring analysts take challenging technical classes such as programming, computer operating systems, network administration, cyberlaw, and security procedures, to name a few. Most of the classes are held in computer labs and are hands-on. Students may also take part in Capture the Flag competitions as part of their course work or as an extracurricular activity. These cybersecurity contests challenge participants to capture and/ or defend computer systems. Taking part in these competitions helps students gain a better view of how malicious hackers operate and demonstrates a candidate's technical skills to prospective employers. A cybersecurity expert writes on Cyber Intern Academy, a website that promotes cybersecurity careers, "Strong performance in Capture the Flag Competitions (CTF) is very important for us and other companies alike . . . [and] can be a significant way to demonstrate if you have the skill for the job."[49] In addition, during their junior or senior year, many students do an internship as part of their studies. Some internships are paid; some are not. Either way, the practical experience gained from an internship is invaluable, as are the contacts that often lead to a full-time position.

Skills and Personality

You can't be an information security analyst and not love computers; nor can you succeed in this job without great information technology skills. In fact, this is a field in which being a computer nerd is a definite plus. British information security analyst Tim Holman explains, "It's a brilliant career for any technically minded person."[50]

Great cybersleuths also have excellent creative problem-solving skills. They enjoy figuring things out and don't back away from a challenge. Information security analysts have to anticipate and respond to complex cyberthreats and fix weaknesses in the system. Since hackers are crafty and technology is continually changing, this often involves coming up with new and creative ways to protect computer systems. Moreover, to ensure they don't miss attempted hacks, analysts must be persistent and pay careful attention to even the tiniest details. Spotting hostile activity is not an easy task, because at any given time there is a vast amount of activity occurring on computer networks. Plus, cyberanalysts have to be lifelong learners who keep up with new and changing technology in order to stay a step ahead of their adversaries.

Working Conditions

As an information security analyst, you'll work in an office environment, spending most of your time in front of a computer. Most information security analysts work full time. Usually, these experts work traditional business hours but are on call in the event of a cyberattack. This means they may have to work nights, weekends, and holidays. Those who are employed by organizations that are open round-the-clock—such as information security firms, health care facilities, and the military—usually work in shifts. Security analysts who work for large companies or consulting firms may travel to different offices within a city or to different cities. These professionals often work in teams with other cybersecurity and information technology professionals.

Employers and Pay

Information security analysts are employed in almost every industry, as well as in government. Many are employed by large health care, financial, insurance, and manufacturing companies. They also work for cybersecurity consulting firms and computer system design firms that provide cybersecurity services to organizations that do not have their own security analysts.

If you pursue this career, you can expect to earn a comfortable living. The Bureau of Labor Statistics (BLS) reports that the median annual wage for information security analysts was $95,510 as of 2017, with the lowest-paid 10 percent earning less than $55,560 and the highest-paid 10 percent earning more than $153,090. Also, analysts typically receive employee benefits, including health insurance, paid sick and vacation days, and retirement benefits.

What Is the Future Outlook for Information Security Analysts?

Currently, there is a global shortage of cybersecurity analysts. And as the threat of cyberattacks increases, so should the demand for information security analysts. The BLS predicts that employment opportunities for these professionals will increase by 28 percent through 2026, which is much faster than average for all occupations. So if you want to make the world a safer place by protecting individuals, industries, and nations from cyberattacks, you should have ample opportunities to do so.

Find Out More
ComputerScience.org
PO Box 524314
Houston, TX 77052
website: www.computerscience.org

ComputerScience.org is an online resource for individuals interested in computer science–related careers. It provides information about a variety of careers, including security analyst; information about degree programs, scholarships, and grants; and interviews with professionals.

Cyber Degrees
website: www.cyberdegrees.org

Cyber Degrees is a website that provides a directory of colleges offering a degree in cybersecurity. It also provides information about different cybersecurity careers, including information security analyst, as well as information about professional certifications and free online courses.

Dark Reading

website: www.darkreading.com

Dark Reading is an online community of information security professionals and a popular cybersecurity news website. In addition to lots of articles, it offers information about new and thwarted cyberthreats, information security careers, the different challenges analysts face, and interviews with information security professionals.

Information Systems Security Association International (ISSA)

1964 Gallows Rd., Suite 310
Vienna, VA 22182
website: www.issa.org

The ISSA is an association of information security professionals, as well as students and others who are interested in this career field. It has chapters throughout the world that offer networking and educational opportunities, Capture the Flag events for students, job postings, publications, and conferences.

Paralegal

A Few Facts

Number of Jobs
About 285,600 as of 2016

Pay
About $31,130 to $81,180

Educational Requirements
Minimum of an associate's degree

Personal Qualities
Interpersonal skills, organizational skills, detail oriented

Work Settings
Indoors in offices and courtrooms

Future Job Outlook
Projected 15 percent job growth through 2026

What Does a Paralegal Do?

Paralegals (sometimes known as legal assistants) are professionals who support and assist lawyers in a variety of ways. One of their primary tasks is locating, gathering, and analyzing mountains of information and documents in order to answer legal questions and obtain facts and evidence related to legal cases. Paralegals also interview clients and witnesses and get affidavits in preparation for court hearings. They write reports that lawyers use in preparation for trials. Plus, they are in charge of filing legal briefs, exhibits, and other applicable documents and items with the court and opposing counsel. Once a trial begins, paralegals assist lawyers by taking notes, organizing and handling documents and exhibits, and reviewing trial transcripts. In fact, it is through the efforts of paralegals that many cases are won. Indiana paralegal Jamie Collins explains, "We do the work. We are in the trenches. We lay the foundation that great cases are built upon."[51]

These legal eagles are responsible for other tasks, too. For instance, they draft legal documents such as contracts, mortgages, and divorce papers. Organizing, managing, and maintaining documents and data as electronic and paper files is still another part of the paralegal's job. Indeed, paralegals do almost everything an attorney does except give legal advice and argue in court. Joseph Spada, director of Paralegal Certificate Studies at Boston University, explains, "Paralegals are now doing the work once done by first, second or third year legal associates [lawyers]. Their work is just as reliable and their billables [fees] are more reasonable which clients appreciate."[52] So if you are interested in the law and want to help others, you might explore a career as a paralegal.

As a paralegal, you can be a generalist who handles all types of legal issues, or you can focus on a particular area of the law. Specialties include, but are not limited to, business, criminal, estate, family, immigration, and real estate law. And you can work in different specialty areas at different times in your career. Jean Cushman, a San Diego paralegal currently specializing in business law, explains, "I started as a generalist and moved to a private firm where I did real estate law. . . . Then one day, real estate died in this area. I needed to find something else to do because I wanted to stay with the firm."[53]

A Typical Workday

Paralegals perform many different tasks. What these professionals do on any given day depends on the cases they are working on, their employer, and their field of specialization. But in general, there are certain activities that are part of almost every paralegal's daily work life. These include conducting research using books, paper records, legal databases, and Internet sites. For example, a paralegal may have to locate and analyze any and all prior cases that are similar to one he or she is currently working on or that contain information pertaining to a specific person, event, or transaction. This often entails searching through thousands of pages of material. Other daily tasks may include organizing paper and electronic files and records, managing databases where records are stored, writing reports, and preparing and reviewing documents for clients and supervising attorneys. Paralegals also attend meetings with attorneys, clients, and witnesses. During some meetings, paralegals help prepare clients and witnesses for cross-examination. As part of this process, they familiarize clients and witnesses with the types of questions that the opposing counsel may throw at them, which helps these individuals avoid making statements that might be used against them. Says Collins, "On most days, I am . . . pushing paper, organizing files, speaking with clients, potential clients, attorneys and court staff, creating pleadings . . . all while attempting to navigate a minefield of deadlines."[54]

During hearings and trials, paralegals organize and handle documents and exhibits, review trial transcripts, and take notes that are shared with the supervising attorney. Collins explains:

There is nothing more satisfying than standing up for a client whose adversary is a big company, police department or some other textbook Goliath in the legal arena. Then there's slipping key notes to your lead attorney during an opposing witness testimony . . . comments written by you to help seal the deal. There's satisfaction in knowing that in that court room on that day at that time . . . there was nothing you could have done any better. You executed everything that came your way like a tactical legal assault ninja.[55]

A paralegal analyzes legal documents in preparation for the next stage in a lawsuit. Paralegals conduct interviews, file legal paperwork, and gather facts into reports—all of which will be used by lawyers for various legal proceedings.

Education and Training

If you are interested in a legal career but are unsure whether you want to invest the time and money that a law degree requires, pursuing a career as a paralegal may be right for you. Paralegals are required to have at least an associate's degree. Some hold a bachelor's degree. Many also obtain voluntary certification, which enhances their chances of advancing in their career. To become certified, candidates must graduate from an accredited postsecondary paralegal program and pass a written exam.

You can start preparing for this occupation in high school by taking the most challenging language arts and speech classes you can manage. Paralegals read through stacks of documents, write reports, draft legal documents, take notes, and interview witnesses and clients, all of which require good communication skills. Language arts and speech classes help you develop critical reading, informational writing, and oral communication skills.

Social studies electives that focus on civil or business law are also useful. They provide aspiring paralegals with a good foundation for postsecondary classes.

Postsecondary paralegal programs introduce students to the legal system. Students are instructed in legal research, writing, theory, and ethics; courtroom procedures; case management; and use of law-specific databases and software, among other topics. Much of the instruction is aimed at giving students practical job skills. For instance, students are taught how to conduct witness and client interviews, draft documents, and perform research. Recalling her course work, Canadian paralegal Jessica Polley says, "We drafted the majority of the documents and materials that I draft on a daily basis. We also would have to file our completed documents with the [mock] 'Court Clerk' as part of our assignments."[56] Many programs require students to participate in an internship as part of their course work. This gives candidates real-world experience working in a law firm, which may also improve their chances of being hired once they graduate.

Skills and Personality

Succeeding as a paralegal takes a variety of skills. Besides having great research and analytic skills, paralegals must have good communication and interpersonal skills. They work closely with lawyers, other paralegals and law firm personnel, clients, and witnesses. Therefore, they should be able to communicate clearly, function as part of a team, and get along with others in an environment where workplace stress can open the door to interpersonal issues. North Carolina paralegal Valerie Chaffin advises, "Maintain civility in the office. It's a landmine for personality conflicts. I think attorneys will find paralegals valuable by the knowledge and experience they have and how they get along with others."[57] In addition, because they deal with a lot of confidential information, paralegals must be trustworthy and discreet.

Being detail oriented is also a must. Overlooking vital information pertaining to a case or making mistakes on documents can result in losing a lawsuit. Organizational skills are important, too. Paralegals often work on many cases simultaneously. They are responsible for maintaining files and documents for every case, keeping these files in order, and retrieving information or documents from them at a moment's notice, tasks that demand organization.

Working Conditions

As a paralegal, you can expect to work indoors in a clean, quiet office setting. You'll also spend time in a courtroom and may travel to other places to interview witnesses or gather information. Most paralegals work at least forty hours a week. Because they frequently have heavy workloads, juggle multiple tasks, and must meet deadlines, paralegals often work overtime. California paralegal Barbara Haas explains, "A typical week will include working through lunch a few days out of the week, and not leaving at 5:00 p.m. until I feel the attorney doesn't need my help."[58] Indeed, the legal industry is high pressure. And this is a fast-paced, challenging occupation. Paralegals typically have lots to keep track of and tight deadlines, which can be quite stressful. Moreover, since paralegals pass on the fruits of their work to lawyers, they do not always receive the personal acknowledgment or respect they deserve, which can be frustrating. However, for many paralegals the rewards of the job outweigh this disadvantage.

Employers and Pay

Most paralegals are employed by law firms, although some work for local, state, and federal governments. Others work for businesses that have in-house legal departments. The Bureau of Labor Statistics (BLS) reports that the median annual wage for paralegals was $50,410 as of 2017, with the lowest-paid 10 percent earning less than $31,130 and the highest-paid 10 percent earning more than $81,180. Pay for overtime hours can add to a paralegal's base salary. Many also receive bonuses based on their

A Rewarding and Demanding Career

"Being a paralegal is a very rewarding career, but it is very demanding. You need to be able to think and react quickly, multi-task, and deal with all types of people. You need to devote yourself to it—it is a career, not just a job. Once you find the right firm, it will be a great career."

—Lori Stewart, US patent paralegal at Fish Richardson PC in Washington, DC

Quoted in Vicki Voisin, "Paralegal Profile: Lori Stewart, PP, PLS," *Paralegal Mentor* (blog), February 17, 2015. www.paralegalmentorblog.com.

performance. In addition, paralegals usually receive employee benefits, including health insurance, paid sick and vacation days, and retirement benefits.

What Is the Future Outlook for Paralegals?

The BLS predicts that employment for paralegals will grow by 15 percent through 2026, which is faster than average for all occupations. So if you enjoy doing research, are fascinated by the legal process, and want to be intellectually challenged, there should be a place for you as a paralegal.

Find Out More

Balance Careers
website: www.thebalancecareers.com

The Balance Careers is a website that provides information about lots of different careers, including that of paralegal. It includes interviews with paralegals; a guide to paralegal education programs, salary, duties, and job skill requirements; and other useful info.

National Association of Legal Assistants (NALA)
7666 E. Sixty-First St., Suite 315
Tulsa, OK 74133
website: www.nala.org

NALA is a professional association for paralegals. Its website provides information about the profession, paralegal education programs, continuing education programs, certification, and networking opportunities.

National Federation of Paralegal Associations (NFPA)
9100 Purdue Rd., Suite 200
Indianapolis, IN 46268
website: www.paralegals.org

The NFPA is a nonprofit professional association made up of paralegal associations. It promotes the paralegal profession and its role in the law industry. Its website offers news, articles, a blog, and publications related to paralegals and information about certification, job postings, and professional development opportunities. The NFPA also sponsors conferences and an annual convention.

State Bar of Texas Paralegal Division
PO Box 19163
Amarillo, TX 79114
website: https://txpd.org

The Paralegal Division is part of the Texas State Bar Association. It represents Texas paralegals. Its website offers information about certification and provides many useful links to Texas paralegal and law associations, federal and state government websites, legal investigative resources, law libraries, and paralegal education programs.

Source Notes

Introduction: Choosing a Career

1. Quoted in Dillion Knight Klackhurst, "Too Many Choices Give Millennials Anxiety," *Huffington Post*, August 18, 2016. www.huffpost.com.
2. Lori Bumgarner, "11 Benefits of Pursuing Your Passions," *paNash* (blog), February 23, 2016. www.panashstyle.com.
3. Siobhan Harmer, "10 Reasons Why Following Your Passion Is More Important than Money," Lifehack. www.lifehack.org.

Data Analyst

4. Quoted in Sarah Royster, "Working with Big Data," *Occupational Outlook Quarterly*, Fall 2013, p. 4. www.bls.gov.
5. Peter Hsu, "A Day in the Life of a Data Analyst," *Carousell Stories* (blog), Carousell, June 27, 2017. https://blog.carousell.com.
6. Quoted in Matt Nollman, "A Day in the Life of a Data Analyst—Featuring Eric Fandel, Data Analyst at Fiksu," Attunity, May 4, 2016. www.attunity.com.
7. Quoted in Ashley Brooks, "What Does a Data Analyst Do? Exploring the Day-to-Day of This Tech Career," Rasmussen College, April 20, 2017. www.rasmussen.edu.
8. Greg DePersio, "Career Advice: Financial Analyst Versus Data Analyst," Investopedia, January 23, 2018. www.investopedia.com.
9. Quoted in Nollman, "A Day in the Life of a Data Analyst—Featuring Eric Fandel, Data Analyst at Fiksu."
10. Quoted in Allison Stadd, "Data Analysts: What You'll Make and Where You'll Make It," *Udacity* (blog), November 26, 2014. https://blog.udacity.com.
11. Quoted in Brooks, "What Does a Data Analyst Do?"

Environmental Scientist

12. Quoted in Greenpeace, "10 Things You've Always Wanted to Ask an Environmental Scientist," April 20, 2017. https://medium.com/greenpeace.
13. Quoted in California Department of Fish and Wildlife, "Featured Scientist: Nicholas Simpson," August 1, 2018. www.wildlife.ca.gov.
14. Quoted in H2M Architects + Engineers, "A Day in the Life of an Environmental Scientist," *Blueprint* (blog), July 10, 2014. https://h2mgroup.wordpress.com.
15. Quoted in California Department of Fish and Wildlife, "Featured Scientist: Mia Roberts," October 12, 2018. www.wildlife.ca.gov.
16. Quoted in Dale Haroski, "Science Notebook: Interview with Kathryn Snead," US Environmental Protection Agency, February 20, 2016. https://archive.epa.gov.
17. Quoted in H2M Architects + Engineers, "A Day in the Life of an Environmental Scientist."

Epidemiologist

18. Quoted in Lauren Weber, "Deadly Hepatitis A Outbreaks Are Exposing Crumbling U.S. Public Health Infrastructure," MSN, December 28, 2018. www.msn.com.
19. Quoted in World Health Organization, "Hunting Ebola in Freetown: A Day in the Life of an Epidemiologist," April 2015. www.who.int.
20. Quoted in Roberta Gibson, "Meet a Scientist Monday: Dr. Minda Weldon, Epidemiologist," *Growing with Science Blog*, May 23, 2009. http://blog.growingwithscience.com.
21. Quoted in Gibson, "Meet a Scientist Monday."
22. Quoted in Gibson, "Meet a Scientist Monday."
23. Quoted in Richard B. Stolley, "A CDC Epidemiologist Talks About Life on the Front Lines of the War Against Ebola," *Time*, November 20, 2014. http://time.com.

Fire Investigator

24. Quoted in Teresa Kay Albertson, "Iowa Fire Marshal Investigates Blaze at Norwalk House," *Des Moines Register*, October 24, 2018. www.desmoinesregister.com.
25. Quoted in West Yorkshire Fire and Rescue Service, "A Day in the Life of a Fire Investigator," May 2, 2015. www.westyorksfire.gov.uk.
26. Quoted in Genevieve Belfiglio, "How to Become a Fire Investigator," Inter Fire Online, 2019. www.interfire.org.
27. Quoted in West Yorkshire Fire and Rescue Service, "A Day in the Life of a Fire Investigator."
28. Quoted in Belfiglio, "How to Become a Fire Investigator."
29. Quoted in Belfiglio, "How to Become a Fire Investigator."

Forensic Accountant

30. Quoted in Forensic CPA Society, "What Is a Forensic Accountant?" www.fcpas.org.
31. Richard Singer, "Forensic Accounting and Famous Cases," Florida Atlantic University, March 25, 2015. https://accounting.fau.edu.
32. Quoted in Insurance News Net, "Careers in Forensic Accounting: It Takes a Sleuth," March 12, 2014. https://insurancenewsnet.com.
33. Quoted in David Mullins, "A Day in the Life of a Forensic Accountant," Axiom Forensics, June 11, 2015. https://axiomforensics.com.au.
34. Quoted in Adam Wade, "A Day in the Life of a Forensic Accounting Specialist," Wiley Efficient Learning, June 27, 2018. www.efficientlearning.com.
35. Quoted in Deanna Arteaga, "Demand for 'CPA Sleuths' on the Rise," Accounting Web, December 23, 2013. www.accountingweb.com.
36. Heinz E. Ickert, "Ethical Considerations for Forensic Accountants," Heinz E. Ickert, LLC, 2016. www.heinzickert.com.
37. Quoted in Arteaga, "Demand for 'CPA Sleuths' on the Rise."

Geological and Petroleum Technician

38. Quoted in Leigh Mceachran, "Dan Carrocci Uses Drilling Knowledge, Geological Skills and Entrepreneurial Spirit to Make Determination Drilling a Success," Fleming College, December 11, 2017. https://flemingcollege.ca.
39. Quoted in Paddy Campbell, "A Day in the Life of Dalradian," *Ulster Herald* (Omagh, Northern Ireland), July 6, 2018. https://ulsterherald.com.
40. Quoted in *WorkBC's Career Trek*, "Geological Technician," Work BC, April 28, 2016. www.careertrekbc.ca.
41. Quoted in Northlands College, "Northern Saskatchewan Training—Geological Technician," YouTube, May 7, 2009. www.youtube.com/watch?v=mzUW6goi4mM.
42. Quoted in Leigh Mceachran, "Earth Resources Technician Co-op Is a Gem for Fleming Graduate Crystal Smith," Fleming College, September 14, 2017. https://flemingcollege.ca.
43. Quoted in *WorkBC's Career Trek*, "Geological Technician."

Information Security Analyst

44. Quoted in Quora, "What Is It Like to Work in Cyber Security?," January 7, 2017. www.quora.com.
45. Quoted in *Education* (blog), "A Day in the Life of a Cybersecurity Expert," NBN, October 14, 2015. www.nbnco.com.au.
46. Quoted in Rutrell Yasin, "A Day in the Life of a Security Analyst," Dark Reading, April 4, 2016. www.darkreading.com.
47. Quoted in Yasin, "A Day in the Life of a Security Analyst."
48. Quoted in *Education* (blog), "A Day in the Life of a Cybersecurity Expert."
49. Quoted in Cyber Intern Academy, "Expert Insights." www.cyberinternacademy.com.
50. Tim Holman, "A Day in the Life of Cyber Security Professional—Tim Holman Writing for Information Week," 2/Sec Consulting, June 16, 2015. www.2-sec.com.

Paralegal

51. Jamie Collins, "Why Did I Become a Paralegal?," *Estrin Report* (blog), June 20, 2011. https://estrinlegaled.typepad.com.

52. Quoted in Chere Estrin, "Meet Joseph Spada: Controversial, Trendsetting Leader, Educator, and Paralegal Career Change Agent," *Estrin Report* (blog), March 21, 2017. https://estrinlegaled.typepad.com.

53. Quoted in Rachel Campbell, "Advice from Experienced Paralegals," *Paralegal Today*, January/February 2004. http://paralegaltoday.com.

54. Collins, "Why Did I Become a Paralegal?"

55. Collins, "Why Did I Become a Paralegal?"

56. Quoted in Leigh Mceachran, "Success Stories—10 Years After High School, Jessica Polley Took the 'Huge, Scary Step' to Attend College," Fleming College, May 23, 2018. https://flemingcollege.ca.

57. Quoted in Campbell, "Advice from Experienced Paralegals."

58. Barbara Haas, "Beyond Brockovich: A Day in the Life of a Paralegal," Fremont College, 2019. https://fremont.edu.

Interview with an Environmental Scientist

William K. Boyes is an environmental scientist specializing in neurotoxicology at the US Environmental Protection Agency in Research Triangle Park, North Carolina. He has worked as an environmental scientist for nearly forty years. He answered questions about his career by email.

Q: Why did you become an environmental scientist?

A: In college, I became intrigued with the way the brain works, in particular in how the brain encodes sensory input that becomes our perceptions of the world, and in using neurophysiological recordings to study brain functions. At about the same time, there was growing concern for environmental pollution, which led to events like the first Earth Day and the formation of the Environmental Protection Agency (EPA). I loved the outdoors, hiking and skiing and wanted to try and help preserve the natural environment. There were relatively few jobs at that time for graduates in neurophysiology or neurobiology, but the environmental field was just opening up. I became aware of neurotoxicology, which concerns effects on the nervous system of exposure to toxic substances, such as environmental pollutants. This combined in one field my two passions; neurobiology and environmental protection.

I went to graduate school at the Department of Environmental Health in the University of Cincinnati and eventually received a Ph.D. in Environmental Health specializing in neurotoxicology. From there I joined the EPA as a postdoctoral fellow and eventually as a principal investigator. I've now worked at EPA for about 38 years doing research primarily on the effects of environmental pollutants on the nervous system.

Q: Can you describe a typical workday?

A: My primary function is to conduct research on EPA priority topics and publish results in the scientific peer-reviewed literature. I typically have two or three active research projects underway at the same time, both in my labs and in collaboration with other scientists. Our primary project currently involves growing cells in tissue culture and exposing them to potential environmental pollutants. We have been studying engineered nanoparticles [microscopic particles] to see if cells will take them up, where they go in the cells, and what aspects of the particles might make them toxic. Most of the hands-on lab is done by students and lab staff. My role is to review their progress and data, discuss what we have learned, what needs to be done next, and work with them to prepare research presentations and manuscripts for publication. I'm also involved in higher level planning of multi-investigator research programs through meetings with EPA regulatory staff—such as those responsible for setting air or water pollution standards. . . . Occasionally, I contribute to major EPA documents such as risk assessments of important chemical contaminants, or reports to Congress on topics such as renewable fuels or hazardous air pollutants.

Q: What do you like most about your job?

A: The best thing about my job is that it gives me a sense of purpose. I firmly believe that protecting the environment is critical for life on our planet, and that my research is one part of a much larger effort to work toward environmental protection. I like that I can both conduct and publish original scientific research, discovering things that no one knew before, and also occasionally have a voice in forming important public health decisions.

Q: What do you like least about your job?

A: Much as I love my job, and I do, the EPA is a part of the large government bureaucracy. There is a dizzying multitude of rules and oversight for virtually every aspect of the operation. These procedures and protocols routinely cause delays that can be very frustrating at times.

Q: What personal qualities do you find valuable for this type of work?

A: The most common factor among those successful scientists I work with at EPA is a deep commitment to the mission of protecting the environment. Obviously, it is important to be intelligent and creative to be a scientist, but it is just as important to be persistent, determined, and self-directed. . . . Being self-directed is also critical to drive an independent research program.

Q: What advice do you have for students who might be interested in this career?

A: Environmental science is a much broader and more diverse field than my corner of environmental neurotoxicology. Environmental science encompasses such fields as: ecology, environmental engineering, analytical chemistry, epidemiology, hydrology, economics, biology, physiology and medicine, computational chemistry, computational biology, exposure science, risk assessment, population dynamics, and urban planning. It also involves interactions with public officials, industrial representatives and decision makers at the community, regional, and national level. My advice to students wanting to work in environmental sciences is to select a related field of specialization for study, such as those listed above, with an eye always to environmental applications.

Q: Do you have anything else to add?

A: Although there have been great improvements in environmental protection over the last three decades, there still is much to be done. . . . The need for young people to work on environmental issues is urgent. For those students who feel this is their calling, there will be no shortage of important problems to address. This will be the challenge of a lifetime.

Other Careers If You Like Research and Analysis

Agricultural scientist
Anthropologist
Archaeologist
Archivist
Astronomer
Atmospheric scientist
Biologist
Chemist
Climatologist
College/university professor
Detective
Economist
Engineer
Financial analyst
Forensic science technician
Forensic scientist
Geographic information
 systems analyst

Geologist
Historian
Hydrologist
Librarian
Marine biologist
Market research analyst
Medical scientist
Operations research
 analyst
Physicist
Public policy analyst
Research psychologist
Sociologist
Software industry analyst
Statistician
Urban planner
Wildlife scientist
Zoologist

Editor's note: The online *Occupational Outlook Handbook* of the US Department of Labor's Bureau of Labor Statistics is an excellent source of information on jobs in hundreds of career fields, including many of those listed here. The *Occupational Outlook Handbook* may be accessed online at www.bls.gov/ooh.

Index